Lions Always Win

How to Spot What You
Want in Business and Life
and Get it Too

Marty Dickinson

The information in this book is based on personal experience and opinion and is intended for general reference and should not be substituted for personal verification by users. The author and publisher disclaim any personal liability for the advice presented on these pages. All effort has been made to verify the accuracy of the information, but we assume no responsibility for errors, inaccuracies, or omissions.

The Snowy Ridge Books Promise:

Our goal at SnowyRidgeBooks.com is to provide you with a proven sequence of steps and sub-steps to learn and apply new skills...faster.

Authors benefit from our process by having a completed non-fiction book to showcase their expertise, in as little as 8 weeks, without ever typing a word of the manuscript.

We have made every effort to produce the content of this book using the exact words provided by the author during a series of intensive content development sessions. The result is a premium quality product in a concise, detailed, format that could have a positive impact on your life if you put its suggestions into action.

c/o Snowy Ridge Books
PO Box 441024
Aurora, CO 80044
www.SnowyRidgeBooks.com
info@SnowyRidgeBooks.com

CONTENTS

SPECIAL FREE BONUS

By purchasing this book, you will be granted access to a password-protected area of our website featuring videos supporting documents, tools, and other valuable resources related to this topic. First, read the book and implement its suggestions. Then, review the instructions in the back of the book for next steps.

IN MEMORIAL

The 2019 passing of Joe Sabah inspired this author to release *Lions Always Win* to the general public instead of only offering its powerful process to clients and family. Joe knew exactly what he wanted, which was to inspire others to share their messages through public speaking. He exercised that desire daily for nearly 40 years by teaching new speakers through his live seminars and by co-founding the Colorado Chapter of National Speakers Association. Not even physical debilitation or age stopped Joe from getting what he wanted. Mostly paralyzed on his left side from a stroke in 2004, he continued to educate audiences for another 14 years. There has never been a better example of a lion who spotted what he wanted and got it too. The world is a far better place because of our departed mentor and friend, Joe Sabah.

INTRODUCTION

Ask anyone, "What do you want?" and you will get just about the same reply every time.

"More vacations."
"Lose weight."
"More money!"

Ask the same people a year later for a progress report, and few, if any, will have attained their stated desires.

With the inundation of books, seminars, speakers, coaches, and therapists focused on the topic of self-improvement, you would think we would all be debt-free, size 3, and money trees by now.

In reality, the opposite is true. A recent survey by Bankrate suggests 29% of people in 2018 had more credit card debt than they had emergency savings. This number had risen eight points from the same survey the year before.

The Organization for Economic Co-operation and Development (OECD) predicted that by this year, 2020, ¾ of the U.S. population would be overweight.

The U.S. Travel Association reported that more than half of employed U.S. citizens surveyed did not even use all of their allotted vacation days last year!

Clearly, most people do not have a clue what they want or how to get it. Something is missing.

While there are many revered authors recognized as industry leaders with decades of track records displaying the perfection we should all want to emulate, I cannot share in that claim. Only recently have I discovered a solution for how to catapult yourself out of a life of mediocrity.

My Hungry Lion Days

Until I was in high school, my parents owned and operated a weekly newspaper in a tiny town, with a population of about 2,000, where we lived in upstate New York. With distribution low and advertisers few, my folks talked of bankruptcy weekly. We never ate at restaurants, and I can count on one hand the number of movies I saw in the theater. I expected little from anyone and anticipated even less for my future.

To my surprise, one day, my parents reached their breaking point and exited the newspaper publishing business. Within weeks, we moved to a mid-sized city in Connecticut. My dad got a sales job that landed him a good salary and provided 6-figure commission checks. My mom got a job as an executive secretary. Suddenly, we had money to spend.

Although all was good on the financial front, I continued to have low expectations for myself. The doubt and lack of faith in myself lasted through high school, college, my first corporate job, and even ten years into ownership of my own business as an internet marketing services provider to other business owners.

One day I realized just how much money my clients had made in their businesses as a result of my team's efforts. Yet, somehow, my own earnings were equivalent to only a mediocre full-time job.

On that same day, I noticed Napoleon Hill's book, *Think and Grow Rich,* sitting on my wife's dresser. I had heard about the book but never read it. Since she was at work, I texted my wife to ask her if I could borrow the book to read. She didn't even know we owned the book or how it ended up on her dresser!

However it showed up in our home, magically or divinely, *Think and Grow Rich* changed my life that day. I started to create my Definiteness of Purpose statement, as the book suggested. I memorized every line and highlighted every page.

Dr. Hill taught me what it meant to <u>describe</u> what one wants and <u>take steps</u> to attain it.

But there was still one problem. I did not know what I truly wanted.

Even more striking was that I discovered my clients had no idea what they wanted either! As I learned more about wanting things and getting them, I

4

started to ask every new client, "What do you *really* want?"

As you can imagine, I would get the same predictable and general responses. "More leads..." or "More sales," were the most common replies.

I had to figure out a way to help my clients determine what they wanted so that I could do my best job of helping them to achieve their goals.

Lions Always Win is the result of that process. It has helped my clients gain clarity on their exact wants and a distinct path toward attaining them. Personally, it has become my go-to system for determining my own desires and realistic expectations for achieving them.

Where you could say I was once a permanent subscriber to mediocrity, I have officially canceled my membership!

Today, you may be feeling like your future is dim or that you've been singled out among your friends and family to live a life of mediocrity. It may seem as though each day is a repetition of the last and that you are not progressing forward. If that's you, I truly understand what you are feeling.

Know right now that an extraordinary life awaits you!

If you own a business and:

- You cannot seem to break through the plateau you have reached
- Your sales and your energy have been going downhill for some time now
- You are worried nothing can turn around your company's progress, then

you have found a virtual partner.

Understand right now that your customers need you and your expertise!

If you are just starting in your adult life and want to avoid the mistakes most people are still making in their 40's, 50's, 60's and beyond, you have found someone willing to share the exact vehicle to help you get anything large or small that you want in life.

Don't wait another year to get started.

Become More Like a Lion

A lion always gets her prey. Sometimes the lion might go a few days without eating meat by supplementing her diet with berries or brush. However, it does not take long before the lion's craving for a feast is so strong that getting what she wants consumes her every intuitive thought and action. No distraction exists for a hungry lion. Lions always win.

Of all predatory animals, the lion may be the closest parallel example to humans, even beyond the gorilla. Lions sleep up to 20 hours a day. Most people would gladly sleep through the days if given a hammock on a quiet beach in the Caribbean without a care in the world.

Lions are slower than the antelope or wildebeest, a lion's favorite meal, and their prey can outrun them. Humans see opportunity every day but are often too slow in making decisions and taking action. The opportunity passes by.

Lions can only run full speed in short bursts. Humans are limited to only a few hours of mentally and physically working at high intensity.

Lions run in packs. Each pack is known as a pride. Humans build pride based on financial and personal accomplishments, and people follow those who accomplish things just like lions in a pack.

The head of a pride is called the head lion. The owner of a successful company is often called a fat cat.

One significant difference between humans and the lion is this: We humans tend to give up quickly if our plans and expectations do not turn out the way we hoped they would. We want results immediately and will gladly pay more for tasks to get accomplished before we even need them. If we aren't satisfied with the results, we move on to another solution and hope for a better result next time.

In short, if you are like most people, you expect to win and win fast. When you don't succeed, or it takes you longer to win at anything, you give up easily.

Lions have no other option. They must eat, at least every few days, or face possible starvation! If lions do not succeed in one hunt, they re-evaluate, reenergize (maybe by taking a short nap), and then resume the chase until they catch dinner.

Again, **Lions Always Win.**

My premise is that you really *do not know* exactly what you want. If you did, and it was important enough for you to acquire, you would already have it by now.

First, this book will help you to figure out why your wants are unclear. Then you will walk through a systematic process to identify your exact wants and prioritize them. At the end of the book, I will introduce you to a simple—and free—method that will all but assure you will have what you want…often much more quickly than you expect to have it.

My Five-Hour Challenge to You

After writing this book, I made my way to a coffee shop at noon on a rainy Sunday. I told my family I would be unavailable by cell phone until I returned. I read the pages of this book and performed the Lion Charges along the way in sequence as if I was going through them for the first time. An honest five hours was the time I needed to complete the program. While this book is arranged in such a way that you can break up your sessions, I challenge you to find, allocate, and commit the time to completing the 12 Lion Charges in one stretch.

Choose a time, either now or in the next few days, where you can be completely alone without distraction for five straight hours. Begin reading the steps in this book and work through the Lion Charges in the order they are presented. By the end, you will complete a specific final activity that I'm betting you have never done before in your life.

You owe this time to yourself, your family, and even to your parents or family that raised you. You also owe this moment of change to your customers or employers, both present and future.

Most importantly, consume this content and complete the Lion Charges (more appropriate than using the word "exercises"), expecting your life to change positively.

Whether you were referred to this book by a friend, or just stumbled upon it, I hope that you come to realize the immense power this tool provides. Please use it wisely and for good reasons.

CHAPTER 1:
FINDING YOUR INNER LION

How did you respond to that information about winning? Were you excited when the word winning was used in the introduction and book title? Or were you offended? Were you a little defensive, thinking this book would be an attempt to justify bulldozing your way through obstacles and people to attain selfish wants at the expense of someone else losing?

I coached my son and his team from his early years of little league baseball to the tournament level. I'm currently coaching my daughter's softball team, depending on the time of the year. One learns a lot about winning when coaching children and what it takes to keep them focused on growth and having a positive experience.

If that's not challenging enough, a youth sports team coach must learn to accept and work with parents teaching their kids those famous cliché phrases like:

"Don't worry about winning; just go have fun out there!"

And my personal favorite: *"There's no I in TEAM."*

At the first practice in the beginning of a new season, before I hear any player or parent repeat these misconceptions, I suggest:

Winning is not everything, but enjoying the game and having fun is sure a lot easier when you're winning.

And,

There might not be an "I" in the word team, but there is an "m" and an "e" and that spells ME. That means you have no control over what any other individual player brings to the game. You can only manage your own desire and willingness to perform at your highest capability. The responsibility is yours and yours alone to want to play to your best ability and contribute to attaining victory.

When you are a business owner, the same is true. Life is a lot more fun when your business is winning! Your spouse is happier. Your in-laws respect you. Your children admire you. You can take vacations and not worry about how sales will be when you return. You can contribute money to charities or pay-it-forward for a stranger at the gas pump. You feel like anything you touch turns to gold! People see in your eyes and energy level that you are doing something right. You walk with confidence and completeness knowing you *won the hunt* in business and life, just like a lion stands with pride over its kill.

Employees tend to wait for others to motivate them through public recognition, pay raises, and advancement. A 2013 Gallup poll suggested 70% of employed staff hate their jobs and that can make getting out of bed in the morning a grueling chore. Winning at work means recognizing there is "no I in team," but not relying on recognition either to motivate your performance. Presenting yourself as a source of self-producing energy and enthusiasm is one of the most important traits anyone can bring to an employer. You must be willing to contribute to assure that your customers remain happy and loyal. That contribution will be your staircase to any position you strive for within the company.

Today, I give you the opportunity to make a truly life changing choice. The first step is to find your inner lion! Remember what it was like on the playground in your school days playing kickball or tag. Whether you were the star athlete or the last one picked for the team, you need to remember what it was like to win!

Lion Charge #1: Feel the Win

Use your watch or cell phone as a timer and give yourself one minute on the clock. On a sheet of paper, I'm going to ask you to finish a sentence that I'm going to start for you. No answer is right or wrong. There is no passing or failing grade. You are not in competition with anyone. It's not a race. And no one knows what you are doing so you don't have to be wondering if this is "cool" or not. This is between you and yourself.

Are you ready?

When you read the statement to yourself, I want you to complete the sentence with a single word, a phrase of words or full sentences. Whatever comes to mind is fine.

The important thing is to not think about it. Just let your pen flow on the paper and write as fast as you can for the entire 60 seconds.

Don't worry about sentence structure or words you choose. Just let it rip. Ready?

Here's the sentence I want you to complete on a sheet of paper:

"When I am winning, I feel _____" (fill in the blank).

GO!

After the minute is up, return to this paragraph.

Hey! Good job. You've taken the first step toward figuring out what you really want in this life and being able to get it too!

Next, I want you to do the same thing with the same sentence. But, this time, I want you to emphasize a single word in the sentence. For this step, emphasize the word "WHEN."

Set your clock for another single minute. When you're ready, say the sentence again to yourself with the emphasis on the word WHEN and repeat the sentence three times.

"WHEN I am winning, I feel…" (fill in the blank).

GO!

If my hunch is correct, you were able to crank out at least a few more descriptions, right? Okay. Now, let's go for one more round. This time, I want you to emphasize only the word "winning."

Remember, set your timer to 60 seconds and then say the sentence to yourself three times with emphasis on the word WINNING.

"When I am WINNING, I feel…" (fill in the blank).

GO!

Congratulations! You have successfully accomplished Lion Charge #1. Write above your list of answers, the title "Winning makes me feel…" so you can identify it when we use it later and put this piece of paper aside for now.

Go refill your coffee or water bottle. There's more to do and you've only been introduced to a small piece of a much larger process you will experience throughout this book.

Win in Time

To compensate for its lack of speed in comparison to the speedy wildebeest feast with legs, the lion must carefully watch her time in the attack. She will find the location of the herd and look for a source of water that her prey is sure to visit. Then, she will immerse herself, hidden and camouflaged, in brown weeds and patiently wait for the tasty treats to cross her path. At the precise moment, she strikes with a vicious chase! Launch too soon or too late and the prey will outrun the predator, leaving the lion to a snack of bush leaves instead of the raw meat she was looking forward to.

Time can be your best friend or worst enemy. In fact, time can be thought of a lot like a bipolar cousin in your family that everyone is nice to but watches closely at family reunions. You just never know when that person will turn on you.

You had to experience the feeling of winning in **Lion Charge #1** so that you could face the challenge of **time**. You have to be very careful with how you view the time you have in a moment, day, week, year or lifetime. Manage your accomplishments with speed and accuracy and time will be on your side. Procrastinate or fall victim to getting sidetracked, and you will soon feel the wrath of time turning against you. Long for that feeling of winning and overcoming challenge will actually become fun along the way.

The secret sauce to keeping time working for you, instead of against you, is to have a strong enough *why*.

Why Do You Want to Do This?

Any student of self-improvement has probably heard that nothing new gets accomplished unless you establish a strong enough *why*. Why is it so important that you reach the goal you're striving to attain? Answering with something like, "I just want more money so I can pay the bills," may be true. But, such a general response is usually not a strong enough *why* to get what you want.

Rest assured that you are going to determine exactly what you want later in the sequence presented in this book. So, try to resist jumping ahead in your thoughts. Focus on your *why* at this very moment.

Is putting your children through college a strong enough *why* to force you to focus on making more money? Is the love for your spouse a strong enough *why* for providing her with a bigger house or a long-awaited vacation? Is walking your daughter down the aisle at her wedding a strong enough *why* for you to finally stop smoking so you live long enough to accomplish that precious event?

As much as you might have heard about establishing a strong enough *why* as your goals motivator, I am here to tell you today that your *why* is the only muscle you have that is strong enough to delay time from its inevitable attack.

Why do I say delay instead of conquering or killing the threat of time? Well, no one lives forever, right? Our calendars of time eventually expire. Most of us will only have mentally and physically productive years until our mid to late 60s and the clock is ticking! All we can do is make the best use of the time we have, in every hour of every day. All of us get 24 hours in a day. Not one of us gets more and none get less. You will need a third of every 24-hour period to involve sleep so that your other two thirds can be productive.

Your *why* is the only force to make you go to bed at 10 p.m. so that you'll be ready to rock the next morning, instead of staying up until midnight having just another drink or two. Your *why* is the only alarm clock that will help you launch out of bed in the morning and race to your computer to start the day instead of hitting the snooze button. Your *why* is the only thing that will trigger your self-motivation to get each business task of your day completed quickly so that you can move onto the next task.

A lion knows her *why* and it never changes.

Students of the book, **Finding Your Why,** by Simon Sinek, will approach this Lion Charge with a bit of skepticism, but let's be clear here. A lion already has a *why*. It always has the same *why*. In fact, a lion's *why* is so laser focused that it never even occurs to her there could be other reasons to invest her entire life into feeding her tribe. The lion is fueled continuously and relentlessly in her search for one thing: contentment.

She longs for that moment when the hunt is complete and the entire pride is stuffed to their fluffy tails with fresh game. Finally, the head lion can find a shady tree and sleep until she can't sleep any more.

To an extent, being content is what we are all after. So, there is at least a little bit of lion in all of us. However, you and I both know people differ from each other. The difference in our *why* is one of those things that makes us who we are.

Discovering your own true *why* is the key to learning more about yourself and what gets you fired up and excited to take action.

You Become Who You Hang Around

Why you think a certain way or take action in one direction and not the other is influenced by the people you have known and spent time with throughout the years. The sound of your laugh, whether or not you pursued college, and how often you joust with people on Facebook about your political opinions are all developed over time based on people you have associated with since childhood.

You have probably heard the saying, "You are what you eat." If you want to get healthy, my suggestion to eat better food would be no surprise. The same goes for people you spend time with. If getting what you want becomes important enough to you, a change in who you hang around and spend time with will be in your near future.

What I am about to say could be the toughest pill in this book to swallow, so I will just get it out of the way now. Getting something you want, that you do not currently have, almost always requires sacrifice of something else.

If you want to lose 100 pounds, avoid going out to eat with friends who love fast food. If you want a successful marriage, spend more time with couples who love each other and enjoy being together instead of those who argue for hours. If you want a promotion at work, stop going to lunch with people at work that spend the whole time voicing the day's drama and start inviting those who you admire in your workplace. If you to want to start a new side-hustle, get to know some business owners who are in the progressing stage of their business instead of spending so much time with friends who tell you your business will fail.

And, yes, if money is what you want, find people who are making good money, increase your time hanging around them and decrease the amount of time you spend with friends who are broke.

When you make the conscious choice to reconstruct what you want in business and life, you must recognize who has been influencing your desires to this point. Take some time now to figure out your *why* by first determining your *who*.

Lion Charge #2: Identifying Your Who

Step 1: On a new piece of paper, draw two lines from the top to the bottom forming three equal vertical columns.

Step 2: Write the names of all the people you consider influencers in your life in some way. You may love them or hate them, but if they have had any impact on you over your lifetime, you need to list them as part of this Lion Charge. Be sure to add your name to the list too!

Your Name
Mother
Father
Son
Daughter
Sister
Brother
Aunt
Uncle
Grandmother
Grandfather
Cousin
(remember that relatives may be biological, step, or adoptive)
Friend(s)
Girlfriend
Boyfriend
Girlfriend's parent
Boyfriend's parent
Girlfriend's friend
Boyfriend's friend

Business Mentor
Business Coach
Colleague
Boss
Mistress
Teacher
Spiritual Leader (e.g. pastor, priest, rabbi, minister)
Therapist
Doctor
God
Others (List all)

Step 3: Using the left column, assign a ranking to each, 1-5, with 1 being most and 5 being least, as to how important that person's opinion of you is. Be brutally honest here and remember no one is going to see these papers but you.

Step 4: Write all names of your #1s into the column on your right in letters twice as big as all the other names (if you don't have five #1s, write your #2s in as well).

Step 5: Circle the five people you feel who have had the most influence on you and your life.

<u>Step 6:</u> To the right of those 5 circled names, and using a ranking of 1-5, 1 being most important and 5 being least important, assign ONE number to each name for how important it is for you to impress that person.

<u>Step 7:</u> Put a big star by the name of the person that you assigned #1. This is the person that has had the **most influence** on your life and is the most important person for you to live up to his or her expectation. That person will likely have an influence in, or even be an actual part of, the development of your *why*.

Your *why* does not only present itself in a person. Your *why* will always be connected to one or more emotions. The emotional component sets the priority for how urgently the *why* must be obtained.

Discovering The Emotions that Dominate Your Actions

Lions have emotions similar to how we experience feelings. You can see the joy on their faces when they win their kill. Their look of utter disgust is obvious when their dinner gets away. The mother lion becomes caring and gentle when comforting her young cubs, but suddenly becomes enraged with anger when unwelcomed visitors come too close to her den.

You and I are the same. We choose to act, or instinctively and often abruptly react, to situations and opportunities based on our emotions.

Here is an example. Let's say your 15-year-old daughter is halfway through her first semester of Spanish class as a high school freshman. You want the best for your daughter. If she can get an A for the course by the end of the semester, you know she will enter the next half of the school year with high confidence.

Great. We've established the "who." Now, let's look at how emotion changes things to arrive at the *why*.

Let's say your daughter has earned an A for all of her exams to this point. Today, she brought home a test where she scored only a B. Do you lock her in her room and ground her until the end of the term so that she does nothing but study to achieve then A? Probably not. A good parent would be sympathetic and patient. "Oh, that was a fluke, honey," you might say. "You will get back up to an A on the next test I'll bet."

Now, suppose your daughter brings a test home one week with a B, and then the next week a test with a C. Would your emotion change? Of course it would.

Perhaps first, you would be surprised. Your daughter has always gotten good grades in school. Then, you would worry about what might be going on at school. Your imagination would run amuck with possibilities! Is she distracted by a boyfriend? Is she hanging around the wrong crowd? What's happened to my perfect daughter?!

Maybe you would avoid going off the deep end like that, but I'm sure you can see that the more intense (or dominant) your emotions become, the higher priority you would place on stopping the downward trend of your daughter's grades.

> # Your person of influence + your dominant emotion = Your Why.

Because your person of influence + your dominant emotion = your *why*, it's important to understand which emotions influence you the most. Your next charge, therefore, will be to identify your dominant emotions.

Note: The National Academy of Sciences provided a convincing study that 27 emotions exist. The results of the study were simplified by author, Katie Avis-Riordan on the CountryLiving.com website (countryliving.com/uk/wellbeing/news/a2454/27-human-emotions-new-study/) where she listed the 27 emotions. I have expanded the list with some additional terms that are connected to the main words of emotion for the purposes of this book.

Lion Charge #3: Identify Your Dominant Emotion

Step 1: On a new piece of paper, draw two lines from the top to the bottom forming three equal vertical columns.

Step 2: Write all of the emotion words on that piece of paper as follows.

Admiration
Adoration
Aesthetic Appreciation
Amusement
Anger
Anxiety
Awe
Awkwardness
Boredom
Calmness
Confidence
Confusion
Contentment
Craving
Desperate
Disgust
Empathetic Pain
Energetic

Entrancement
Envy
Excitement
Fear
Giving
Happiness
Horror
Interest
Joy
Nostalgia
Pride
Relaxation
Resentment
Romance
Sadness
Satisfaction
Sexual Desire
Supportive
Sympathy
Triumph

(List any variations of emotion words that are more appropriate to you. For example, maybe you would rather use the word Happy instead of Excitement).

Step 3: Using the left column, assign a ranking to each 1-5, with 1 being most and 5 being least, as to how consuming each emotion is for you.

For example, some people seem to be sad all the time, even when positive things happen in their lives. Any negative occurrence in the day drags them deeper and deeper into a pit of despair. Sadness consumes their every thought and debilitates them from taking any action toward a happy, positive outcome. In this case, Sadness would receive a "1" for ranking.

Many people are the opposite. They see the positive in everything. The only time sadness invades their positivity is with the death of a close relative or friend. Even then, the mourning time is short and their positive outlook resumes. In this case, Sadness would receive a "5" for ranking.

Get to know yourself with these emotions. Many of these words have multiple definitions. Spend some time researching each definition using Dictionary.com and select which definition is most fitting, and triggering, for your emotion and then assign a ranking.

Be brutally honest here and remember that no one is going to see these papers but you.

Step 4: Write all of your #1s into the column on your right in letters twice as big as the other emotions (If you don't have five #1s, write your #2s in as well).

Step 5: Circle the top five emotions that consume your thoughts.

Step 6: To the right of those five circled emotions, select which emotion will be given a 1, 2, 3, 4, or 5 with 1 being the most consuming and 5 being least consuming emotion.

Step 7: Put a big star by the emotion for which you assigned #1. This is your **dominant emotion** that moves you to action more than any other!

Assembling Your Whys

Napoleon Hill in his legendary book, *Think and Grow Rich*, stated how important it is to identify your Definiteness of Purpose, as he called it. In some parts of the book, he referred to this phrase to describe your ultimate goal in life. Other times, he used it to suggest having definiteness of purpose for minor desires as well.

Your *why* can take multiple forms as well. You can have a main *why* that you use to base all decisions and prejudge all actions. *Whys* can be tiny, and not thought of often, but they still exist and contribute to the choices you make.

Lions understand this concept all too well. Their overall *why* is a combination of their main *who* (themselves) and *contentment* (emotion resulting from a full tummy).

Wildlife specialists would probably argue that a lion's main *why* is the tribe itself. In reality, protecting and serving the tribe is the lion's *definiteness of purpose*, not its true *why*. Its *why* is the driving force for risking its life to protect the tribe and keep it nourished.

You, too, have an overall *why* that dominates your every action. Then, you have small *whys* and several in the middle. Your next step is to combine your *whos* with your *emotions* to arrive at your prioritized *whys*.

Lion Charge #4: Identify Your Main *Why*

<u>Step 1:</u> On a new piece of paper, write the names of all the top five people you chose as main influencers in your life and list them vertically from 1 through 5 in order of importance. Give enough

space between each name so that your 3rd name is in the middle of the column and your 5th name is near the bottom, with equal space between each name.

Step 2: Refer to your list of your top five emotions. When you think of each person, which of the top five emotions are associated with that person? Write those emotions to the right of the person's name. Use big letters to help your top five emotion words stand out.

Step 3: What other emotions from your original list can be associated with this person? Write them in the remaining space next to each person's name, but write them in smaller size than your top five emotions.

Step 4: Circle any name to which you added your #1 dominant emotion. Don't be too surprised if you find that emotion word next to all of your top five influencer names.

Step 5: Make a large rectangle to outline the person's name and the emotion words for which you have the most emotions listed, including your #1 dominant emotion. You have just discovered your main *why*. All of the others are certainly relevant, but will most likely be at least slightly smaller in rank from the main *why*.

Refer to your list of **How Winning Makes Me Feel** from Lion Charge #1. Only with a strong enough *why* can you even expect yourself to figure out what you truly want or have enough energy and focus to get what you want. If you are reading this book and hear me speaking directly to you, then please receive this suggestion with an open mind:

Stop beating yourself up for not knowing what you want or not getting what you want and start thinking of what is truly important to you and, most importantly, *why*.

Introducing Your Mystery Leader

As I mentioned earlier, a lion lives with a group of other lions, called a pride. There is a dominant male and a dominant female to lead the group and maintain order within the pride. In the rare event that opposition arises, the challenger is immediately identified and dealt with quickly and swiftly.

Whether you are the CEO of a company with thousands of employees, a brain of one as a sole proprietor, or just got hired as an intern delivering coffee to cubicles, you are the dominant lion in your very own pride. But there is one essential differentiator between your executive round table and a lion's pride: You have a mystery leader on your team. And you are probably not even aware of him until now.

Oh yes, he exists. He rides with you on the train or in your car on your way to work. He's present at all the team meetings, even though you might not hear him speak up. He listens to every customer service phone call, but you'll never hear him enter the conversation. He accompanies every sales presentation, but stands in a dark corner of the room observing. He watches over your website designers and hovers over programmers while they write their code. He never guides them, however, to complete the project in a certain way.

This board member has such a profound impact on you that he should have a job title and description with a pay grade! Indeed, he is costing you money as if you really are paying his salary.

For the purposes of this book, I'm going to assign this mysterious board member the title of **CEB or Chief Executive Bully** and will refer to it frequently throughout this book. I've used the word "bully" because that's exactly what this mystery leader does. Every time you come up with a good idea, this bully *in your mind* cuts you down, laughs at you, and tells you, "What a stupid idea!"

Your CEB has been awarded rank of Chief Executive because he's right at the top of your subconscious mind. Everything you do gets passed through the CEB for approval. And if he doesn't like what you present, it gets thrown out before the rest of the board can even vote on the action.

Big Problems Have Deep Roots

Your CEB has been with you probably for a long time, even before you started your business or completed your first resume. In fact, I'm going to go out on a limb that, for most readers of this book, your CEB has existed since you were a young boy or girl.

This CEB has been influencing your decisions from grade school and high school straight through to your dating preferences and marriage all the way to your current career and family practices. With that kind of influence in your life for so long, you would find it easier to break off an engagement with your fiancé than to say goodbye permanently to your CEB.

In fact, I cannot promise total elimination of your CEB as even a possibility, and you may even require professional help to fully confront any early childhood trauma. That is not the purpose or goal of this book.

There is a great book on Amazon by a 30-year therapist. Her name is Susie Hayes and her book is titled, **FREED from Stuck: Dare to Cross the Bridge Beyond Grief, Trauma, and Self-Sabotage to Discover Lasting Change Now**. She uses the example of a piece of furniture with a scratch on it to illustrate what holds people back from achieving what they want in life. She says, "The part that is stopping you from succeeding at your goals is just a part of you. It is not what makes you uniquely you and special."

What holds you back, Susie says, is equivalent to the scratch on the dresser. You would not throw away a beautiful chest of drawers just because it had a little scratch on it, would you?

Commit at this moment to do whatever it takes to reduce your CEB's dominance over your thoughts and actions. Think of it like giving your CEB a demotion. You will know he's still there but maybe reduced to a part-time laborer without much influence on your new direction.

Wait! Where Are You Going? Come Back!

Please do not jump ahead in this book or get sidetracked. That's usually what happens when people are confronted with the idea of recognizing their CEB. In fact, any attempt to put this process off until later is a direct attempt by your CEB to prevent you from succeeding with this process!

Do not let the temptation get the best of you. You didn't just pick up your CEB this morning like a flu bug! Your CEB has taken years to cultivate and inflame so that it has literally restricted you from getting beyond the plateau you've found yourself in.

You need to be introduced to the solution using a step-by-step method so that you are truly inspired and excited enough to take IMMEDIATE action with it. But, you have to be ready to accept that solution before you can implement it.

LIONS ALWAYS WIN by Marty Dickinson

CHAPTER 2:
SURVEY YOUR DOMAIN

If you could only pick one thing you are really good at, and I mean truly exceptional, could you describe it to me? Most people are extremely lucky to be highly skilled at even one task. Even if someone claims to be a jack of all trades, very rarely will you find someone truly outstanding in more than one or two areas of skill.

The same is true for your weaknesses. When I started my first company in 1995, I woke up on Monday morning of the first week after I quit my job realizing I needed to immediately become an expert in about 40 different things. I knew that was impossible. So, I made a list of all 40 things and decided then and there what I had an interest in learning versus those components of owning a business that I knew I would never learn.

What multitude of skills will you choose to never learn and get good at? What essential components of managing and growing a business will you be willing to learn so that you know enough to hire the right person to perform those tasks for you? What skills can you offer an employer so that you can bring value to the company within the first week of your employment?

Lion Charge #5: Discover What You Are Really Good at and be Honest with What You Will Never Want to Do.

Here is a quick way to assess what you're good at, what you need to learn (or have a desire to improve upon), and what you expect to NEVER learn how to do on your own.

Step 1: On a separate piece of paper, draw two vertical lines so that you have three vertical columns of equal width.

<u>Step 2:</u> Hand-write the word or phrase for each of the following skills down the middle column.

Ability to calculate numbers and dollars in your head

Accounting

Analyzing someone's body language in an in-person meeting

Computer Maintenance (Hardware Repair)

Confidence

Content creation (blog posts, articles)

Creating a marketing plan

Creativity

Determining pricing of products or services

Editing images or photos for size and format

Excel or MAC spreadsheets

Focus

Gathering facts and making prompt decisions

General computer skills

Grammar and punctuation

Listening to others talk and showing interest

Locating funding

Managing people

Media experience (radio, t.v. podcasts, webinars)

MS Word or MAC word processing

Multitasking capability

Organization skills

Patience with others

Patience with yourself

Pay-per-Click or PPV advertising

Photography

Pleasant and welcoming physical appearance

PowerPoint

Preparing a financial budget

Press release writing

Product creation and development

Project management

Public speaking

Remembering peoples' names after you meet them

SEO (Search Engine Optimization)

Sales copywriting

Selling in-person

Selling on the phone

Selling products on the web

Selling services on the web

Social networking (Facebook, LinkedIn, Twitter, Instagram)

Speed of task completion

Statistical analysis

Talking with people on the phone

Training people

Troubleshooting computer problems

Typing speed

Understanding legal contracts

Video creation

Video editing

Voice quality on the phone

Web programming (CSS/PHP/MySQL)

Website design

Writing etiquette

If you know there are additional skills needed to be successful in your particular business, industry, or career, list them too.

Step 3: In the column on the left, assign a number to each word or phrase based on the descriptions below:

1=I rock! No one I know is better at this task than I am and I could do this all day long and never get sick of it.
2=I'm no rookie at this but I still have to work at it.
3=I'm just getting started but show promise.
4=Don't make me do this on my own today, but maybe someday.
5=No Chance! If you make me do this, I will quit or close my business.

Step 4: Rewrite the words or phrases in the right column, but this time write all of your #1s at the top, then all of your #2s under the #1s, then all of your #3s under the #2s until the list is complete with all of your #5s at the end.

Step 5: Circle "one" of the words for which you are the most highly skilled.

Put this paper on top of the Lion Charge #1 paper you completed earlier as you will use it further along in this book.

All of these questions are leading up to the vital question to ask yourself that turns out to be the one thing almost all business owners neglect to identify, which I will reveal momentarily.

If you have faithfully read this book to this point, without jumping ahead, congratulations! Thanks for granting my request. My teasing has been for good reason as you shall soon see. If you skipped to this section, I urge you to **stop your eyes from wandering** and return to where you left off and continue reading...until you have earned the right to be at this point in the process.

Take a look at your two completed pieces of paper for a moment. Look at one of the emotions from Lion Charge #1 and compare it with your #1s and #2s of the Lion Charge #5 list. You should start to see some similarities and contrasts.

Which of your skills can you most associate in your mind with winning?

What emotions of winning are most easily achieved when you perform certain tasks?

You do not need to write down your answers to those questions. Instead, allow your conscious brain to connect the thoughts with your subconscious. Don't worry, your subconscious is way ahead by making literally hundreds of connections for you already.

Hopefully, you will have plenty of energy to keep going in this process knowing your brain is helping you. Contrary to what you may have been convinced of by your CEB, your brain really does want you to succeed and get everything you want in this life. All you have to do is welcome your brain to join your team.

Go get another cup of coffee or fill your water jug. Be sure to stand up and walk around for a couple of minutes. When you return, be ready and confident to figure out what you truly want. Are you ready?

LIONS ALWAYS WIN by Marty Dickinson

CHAPTER 3:
SPOTTING WHAT YOU REALLY WANT

Go ahead and admit it. You do not really know what you want. How can I be so sure of this fact? And, how can I be so confident that 99.5% of people reading this book will privately agree with that statement if they are honest?

The answer is because over the past six years, I have asked every new client and business acquaintance the following question: "What do you want?" Only 12 people (out of around 600) have ever been able to provide me with a detailed response.

How could you ever expect to gain any traction starting or expanding a business without a clear understanding of what the business will need to grow and what you will want to get out of the deal?

Only after you identify exactly what you want, can you craft a plan to get you there.

Where Do You Want to Go Today?

When you start your car in the morning and press the accelerator pedal, how will you ever arrive at a chosen destination unless you think about where you want to wind up? Driving to your grocery store down the block is much different than taking a five-day trip across the country.

Operating a business or climbing the corporate ladder is similar to driving your car. You have to know exactly where you want to wind up before you accelerate! I'm going to show you how.

Avoiding Fool's Wants

A WordPress developer I've been working with asked me the other day, "How can I get more clients?" My response was this: "That never works. You have to be much more detailed when describing what you truly want."

More sales, more leads, more clients, more skilled helpers, lower costs, higher profit margin. Just like a miner is misled by fool's gold, I consider all of these examples to be "fool's wants."

Does the lion start running aimlessly the moment she decides she is hungry and wants to hunt her dinner? No! she selects a location and position to gain her advantage, due to her lack of speed in comparison to the antelope and wildebeest, and then patiently waits to see what herds of prey start to gather around a water hole. Finally, she carefully spots her victim (very specifically) and attacks by way of surprise.

If my claim is true that you really do not know what you truly want, I can bet you have been living on **fool's wants** for much of your professional and personal life. You may be able to look back to your childhood and teen years and remember fool'js wants you wished for as well (grow taller, get better at basketball, have a girlfriend or boyfriend, get a job).

Again, I suggest you try not to be too hard on yourself if you are just realizing now how destructive your thinking has been to your business and life progress over the years. Your parents, siblings, friends and even teachers likely had no idea how to coach you in this area. Just consider yourself fortunate that someone is bringing it to your attention now. So, let's move forward!

How to Figure Out Exactly What You Truly Want

I will now take you through three steps to help you discover what you really want. Each want could start out with something very simple and even bordering on fool's wants, as described earlier, such as a new car, a spouse, freedom to spend more time with your aging mother or to cure cancer. You will start there and work your way to **true wants**. Whatever it is you truly want, whether large or small, the process to discovery is the same. Those three Want Discovery Steps are as follows:

1.   Define your current self-culture image
2.   Describe what you DON'T want
3.   Expand on what you DO want

Lion Charge #6: Create Your Current Self-Culture Image

You have probably heard how wonderful it is to work for a company like Google. Free food is provided in their cafeteria. Employees ride skateboards down the hallway. Foosball tables are in every playroom free for everyone to use. These are all symbols of Google's corporate culture.

Taking an inventory of your own self-culture, as it is today, is the first step in discovering how you want to craft your professional and personal life in future years. For each category, write at least one sentence to identify a success and another to describe what you feel is a failure in that area.

Once again, take out a new sheet of paper and write down every one of these categories. Write your successes in the left column and failures in the right.

Business: Describe the current status of your business or employment.

Success:	Failure:

Finance: Describe your current debt situation and income.

Success:	Failure:

Assets: Describe your home, car, toys, possessions.

Success:	Failure:

Education: How pleased are you with your past education?

Success:	Failure:

Time Management and Productivity: How well do you spend your day?

Success:	Failure:

Work Ethic/Self-Motivation: How do you approach your work?

Success:	Failure:

Associations: Who do you hang around and spend time with?

Success:	Failure:

Influence: Who do you have an impact on?

Success:	Failure:

Respect and Admiration: Who respects and admires you?

Success:	Failure:

Recreation: What do you do for fun?

Success:	Failure:

Family: Do you enjoy their company and is spending time with them a priority?

Success:	Failure:

Health: Are you ill most of the time or well? Describe your general health.

Success:	Failure:

Love: Do you feel loved and do you share your love in return?

Success:	Failure:

Sex: How often do you have sex and how sexually fulfilled are you?

Success:	Failure:

Vacation/Time Off: How often do you take time off?

Success:	Failure:

Travel: Do you get to travel a lot and do you enjoy traveling?

Success:	Failure:

Recreation: Describe your downtime.

Success:	Failure:

Safety: Describe how safe and secure you feel in your home and life in general.

Success:	Failure:

Spiritual/Religious: Describe your time/activities devoted to worship, study, or practice.

Success:	Failure:

Giving/Charity: Describe your contributions of time and money to charity.

Success:	Failure:

Childhood: What events impacted you positively and negatively?

Success:	Failure:

Now, on a new sheet of paper, assign an overall ranking from 0-10 to each of the categories.

10 = This part of my life needs no improvement and is perfect!

0 = This topic is completely non-existent or sorely in need of improvement!

Category	Ranking 0-10
Business	
Finance	
Assets	
Education	
Time Management and Productivity	
Work Ethic/Drive/Self-Motivation	
Associations	
Influence	
Respect and Admiration	
Family	
Health	
Love	

Sex	
Vacation/Time Off	
Travel	
Recreation	
Safety	
Spiritual/Religious	
Giving/Charity	
Childhood	

Lion Charge #7: Describe What You Don't Want

Your next step in discovering what you truly want is to create a list of things you want to avoid. On a new sheet of paper, answer the following questions. No answer is too short or too long.

WARNING!! Be ready! Your brain is already trying to help you avoid this step because it wants to protect you. Do NOT seek an alternative to writing your answers by hand on paper. Your brain needs to connect with what you are thinking and writing. Do NOT jump ahead and start creating what you DO Want. Staying with the process is crucial here!

Use the list of categorized successes and failures above as a starting point. Refer to your rankings as well.

What I Don't Want to Happen with My Business

What I Don't Want for My Finances

What I Don't Want to Happen with My Assets

What I Don't Want to Happen with My Education

What I Don't Want My Time Management and Productivity to be Like

What I Don't Want My Work Ethic/Drive/Self-Motivation to be Like

Who I Don't Want in My Associations Anymore

How I Do Not Want to Influence Others

What would cause those you care about to NOT respect and admire you?

Recreational Activities I Do Not Want to Take Part in

What I Don't Want to Occur in My Family

What I Don't Want My Health to be Like

What I Don't Want in My Love Life

What I Don't Want My Sex Life to be Like

What I Don't Want in My Vacation Time or Time Off

What I Don't Want in My Travel Plans

What I Don't Want in Regards to My Personal Safety

```



```

What I Don't Want in My Spiritual or Religious Future

```



```

What I Don't Want in My Giving/Charity/Volunteer Life

```



```

What I Don't Want from My Childhood to Influence or Dominate My Adult Life

```



```

Lion Charge #8: Describe What You Do Want

You might have guessed that the next step in the process is to turn your non-wants into wants. That might work for some categories of your life. But, it's not a golden rule. Again, try to restrain yourself from just jumping ahead. It took years and years to get your life to this point of not knowing what you truly want. Invest just a few more minutes reading the following background and instructions for this step so that you work through it properly and completely.

One of my web marketing mentors is Armand Morin. One of his non-web marketing events was held in Las Vegas with the focus of reaching one's full potential.

After a few hours of introductory content, he had us perform an exercise that was pretty eye opening to the group by the time it was complete. He assured us what we were about to do would be held in strictest confidence and privacy.

Armand simply asked a question, for which we were supposed to reply with written answers on a piece of paper that only its author would see. The question was:

"What do you want?"

Everyone seemed to be writing so feverishly. I sat there with a dull look on my face that made me think of the human astronaut in the original Planet of the Apes movie that had a portion of his brain removed as part of the standard lobotomy procedure given to humans as punishment for speaking.

After about ten minutes of silence in the room of 150 people, and me with absolutely nothing written on the piece of paper in front of me, he said it again but in a slightly different manner.

"What do **YOU** want?"

I wrote down a few things like more vacations per year, more money, more family time, y'know, the basics that probably most Americans would recite.

Then, he said it again:

"What do you **WANT?**"

A few more ideas made it to my mostly white piece of paper.

After another five minutes or so, he asked one final question. Can you guess what his question was? I'll bet you're right! He said with new emphasis on the first word:

"**WHAT** do you want?"

Armand was really on to something. He conveniently proved to those of us who had no clue what we really wanted that we could muster a few wants onto paper.

The exercises provided a convenient, and almost pompous, way for about half the group to demonstrate to others around them that they had it all together and knew exactly what they wanted to achieve in life.

Honestly, I felt a bit intimidated because I really did not know what I wanted. In that time of my life, I was working seven days a week. Usually, I would put in 12-16 hours of work time a day. I simply had no time to really think about dreams or aspirations. Well, that's what I thought anyway.

If you have no time to think about what you want, that should be a red flag 911 emergency alert that you have to stop whatever you are doing at that point and just disappear for a day. Figuring out what you want is not only the most important thing you can do toward the success of your business but also for the attainment of a fulfilled life!

Anyway, back to the story of the Armand event. When I was later matched up with a few of those attendees with the perfectly calculated lives during later exercises, I learned that even the confident people were just as lost as the rest of us. Almost none of us in the room could articulate what we really wanted in this precious life of ours.

Again, I ask...How can we as business owners or future C-Suite executives achieve success if we cannot even articulate what it is we want?

I certainly do not want to take anything away from Armand's event. In fact, I highly recommend you attend any live Armand Morin conference. What I'm attempting to do is incorporate one of his helpful exercises into a more complete process I've developed over time.

 **Notice: If you have NOT worked through the prior Lion Charges in this book please do not cheat yourself! Go back, grab some paper and start writing.**

With steps #1 and #2 complete, refer back to your successes and failures as well as your non-wants to create True Wants for each category below. To spur your thoughts even further, use Armand's technique and ask yourself, out loud, each question using emphasis on all five main words to stimulate your thinking.

What Do I Want for...my (Topic)? Fill in the blank with the category name.

What Do I Want for...my (Topic)?

What do I Want for...my (Topic)?

What do I Want for... my (Topic)?

What do I Want for My (Topic)?

After you ask each question, for each category, one category at a time, give your mind some time to think. Say the same question again a few times with the same inflection to give your brain room to breathe.

Write your answers with great detail and do not be afraid to use several pieces of paper for this portion of the Lion Charge. Use the large boxes first to brainstorm your answers. Avoid the temptation to just write "more money" in the Finances box. Describe exactly how much money you simply must have and by what date you must have it, for example. Don't just write "new house" in the Assets box. Describe it as it looks in your mind as you drive up to the front door and park. What does the lawn look like? What color is the front door? When you open the door, what kind of floor is there? Is there a stairwell to the right or do you just walk straight ahead to the kitchen?

 **Notice: The Wants questions have changed in order from the "Don't Wants" you answered earlier. The reasoning is very important as you will soon understand. Be sure to answer the Wants questions in the sequence provided.**

After you have brainstormed a category, use the following smaller box to write a condensed version of the Want. Your condensed Wants should be less than 20 words.

Hopefully, you have an idea of the kind of detail I am expecting. Your answers could possibly fit in the boxes provided for some of the questions. Or, you could find yourself writing a page or more for just one answer! Limitations do not exist here. Be detailed. Let your mind run free!

Now it is your turn. Go!

What Do I Want for Vacation or Time Off?

What Do I Want for Vacation or Time Off? Condensed 20-Word or Less Version:

Do the same for the rest of the categories in this order:

What Travel Opportunities Do I Want and Where Do I Want to Travel?

How Do I Want My Health to Improve?

How Do I Want to Spend My Recreational Down Time?

What Do I Want for Assets (House, Car, Boat, Toys)?

How Do I Want to Influence Others?

WHO Do I Want to Respect Me and Admire Me and for What?

WHO Specifically or What Type of People Do I Want to Association With?

What Do I Want to Change in My Family?

What Do I Want for My Love Life?

What Do I Want for My Sex Life?

What Do I Want for My Personal Safety?

What Do I Want for (Create your own spiritual or religious statement here)?

What Financial Contribution or Time Do I Want to Give to Charity?

What I Do I Want to Keep With Me from Childhood as an Adult?

What Do I Want for My Time Management and Productivity?

What Do I Want for My Work Ethic/Drive/Self-Motivation?

What Do I Want for Education and Continued Learning?

What Do I Want for My Finances?

What Do I Want for My Business?

Well done! You should now have several pages of what I call Want Statements from this list, even if you originally thought you didn't want *anything*, or, more likely, you simply did not *know* what you truly wanted. Nearly everyone that goes through this Lion Charge is amazed at how many Want Statements they produce.

LIONS ALWAYS WIN by Marty Dickinson

CHAPTER 4:
ASSIGNING SPECIFIC PLANS TO GET WHAT YOU WANT

If you continue to work seven days a week, and one of your wants is to go to church every Sunday with your family, you will not have a positive outcome. If one of your wants is to take three two-week vacations per year, but you refuse to hire your first full-time helper, you will probably never even get to enjoy one vacation per year—unless you wind up working through the whole vacation.

The next sequence I would like you to work through is probably going to be the most challenging part of the program. If you have not refilled your coffee cup in a while, or taken a stretch break, now would be a good time to do that.

Remember in Lion Charge #5 where I had you assign numbers 1-5 to identify your areas of expertise for a various business and personal skills?

Now, you will revisit those answers and create what I call "Get Statements."

A Get Statement is what needs to be done to accomplish, earn or acquire a Want.

Lion Charge #9: Create Get Statements

Here is the process, in summary, for what I will ask you to do:

1. Condense your detailed wants descriptions for each category into single one-liner sentences and add them to the left column.
2. Choose from your list of business and personal skills and describe what has to happen to fulfill the "Get."

Here is an example to show you exactly what I mean. Imagine that one of my "Wants" is to stop hackers from breaking into my computer because I am highly paranoid of having my identity stolen. Let's also imagine that I answered the skills category near the beginning of Lion Charge #5 under Computer Maintenance as "No Chance!" The fact that I chose No Chance means I'm not willing to learn how to fix my computer myself. So, my "Required to Get" will involve paying someone to come in and fix my computer.

Here is how I would complete this sequence:

Category: Personal Safety Want

Want	Required to Get
Prevent hackers from breaking into my computer and stealing my identity.	Find and pay a security expert to evaluate my computer, scan code for malware, install the correct virus protection software, fix and lock-down.

You will find nearly every one of your "Wants" is attainable with the right people and expertise at your side. Of course, let's not leave education out of this equation. You are much smarter than you give yourself credit for! You could learn just about anything if you really *wanted* to and with the proper instruction.

Therein lies the key: Some things you just do not have an interest in learning or are unwilling to invest the time to learn at this time in your life.

Again, *your* turn has arrived. On a new sheet of paper:

1. Create a narrow column on the left titled Want
2. Create a wide column on the right titled Required to Get
3. Shorten each condensed 20-word or less Want from Lion Charge #8 into even shorter specific one-liners and write them in the narrow left column. This will become your official list of True Wants.
4. In the wide right column next to each Want, write in detail what you feel needs to happen for the Want to be implemented fully. These will be your "Required to Get"

pre-plans, which will be used later in the process.

Some of these Wants and Required to Gets may conjure some emotions as you go through them. The papers you are writing on can be kept as confidential as you would like them to remain. Let your fingers run wild! Circle money numbers. Underline important words. Use exclamation points! Bold important words. Allow your mind to control how you write these Want statements.

Remember: Don't try to stuff 10 Business Wants into one box, for example. Individualize everything— Apply one Required to Get for every individual Want. Sure, you could write out 10 Business Wants in a row, but provide a single Required to Get for each individual want.

Category: Vacation/Time Off Want

Want	Required to Get

Category: Travel Want

Category: Health Want

Category: Recreation Want

Category: Assets Want

Category: Influence Want

Category: Respect and Admiration Want

Category: Association Want

Category: Family Want

Category: Love Want

Category: Sex Want

Category: Personal Safety Want

Category: Spiritual/Religious Want

Category: Giving/Charity Want

Category: Childhood Want

Category: Time Management and Productivity Want

Category: Work Ethic/Drive/Self-Motivation Want

Category: Education Want

Category: Finance Want

Category: Business Want

Lion Charge #10: Rank Your "Required to Get" Action List

How can you know which action items to accomplish first? Fortunately, that question can be answered pretty easily with a simple ranking system.

Rank each of your "Required to Get" items based on cost, ease, speed, personal feeling/emotion (**your why**), and expected ROI (return on investment) between numbers 1-5. This is the same ranking criteria I use for my 101 Realistic Website Traffic Methods (101TrafficMethods.com) whitepaper and it works terrifically for this purpose as well. I'll describe each of those specifically for you:

Cost: Can this "Required to Get" be implemented for free? (Rank=1)

Or,

Will it cost a ton of money to accomplish, learn, or acquire? (Rank=5)

Ease: Can this "Required to Get" be implemented easily? (Rank=1)

Or,

Will you need to go through great lengths and spend hours of your own time and mental anguish to accomplish, learn, or acquire this Get? (Rank=5)

Speed: Can this "Required to Get" be implemented quickly? (Rank=1)

Or,

Will it demand several months or even years to accomplish, learn, or acquire? (Rank=5)

Personal: This Want is my highest personal priority! (Rank=1)

Or,

This Want is of no importance to me at all. (Rank=5)

ROI: What is the potential return on investment of your finances, time, or mental peace for this "Required to Get?" Is there a great financial reward possibility even though you only spent 10 minutes implementing this Get on your own? (Rank=1)

Or,

Will this action require Super Bowl advertising rates with only a small amount of actual sales in return? (Rank=5)

 **Remember: Rank items as 2, 3, and 4 when the "Required to Get" is not at the extreme ends of the ranking spectrum.**

Ready? Go!

Vacation/Time Off Want Description: _____

_____

Required to Get	Cost	Ease	Speed	Personal	ROI	Total

Travel Want Description: _____

_____

Health Want Description: _____

_____

Recreation Want Description: _____

_____

Asset Want Description: _____

_____

Influence Want Description: _____

_____

Respect and Admiration Want Description: _____

_____

Associations Want Description: _____

_____

Family Want Description: _____

_____

Love Want Description: _____

_____

Sex Want Description: _____

_____

Safety Want Description: _____

_____

Spiritual/Religious Want Description: _____

_____

Giving/Charity Want Description: _____

_____

Childhood Want Description: _____

_____

Time Management and Productivity Description:

_____

Work Ethic/Drive/Self-Motivation Want
Description: _____

_____

Education Want Description: _____

_____

> **Note: Your Finance Want Descriptions may have varying time frames in which to achieve them. For this reason, we have expanded the grid to include short term as well as long term Wants.**

Finance Want Description: _____

_____

Required to Get	Cost	Ease	Speed	Personal	ROI	Total
Now:						
Next Month:						
Next Quarter:						
By 6 Months:						
By 9 Months:						
By 12 Months:						

Business Want Description: _____

_____

Lion Charge #11: Prioritize Your "Required to Gets" into an Implementation Order

This next step is my favorite of all the Lion Charges because you really start to see how your "Wants" can become "Gets." It starts to seem doable!

Simply write all of your lowest ranked "Required

to Get" items in the list below and continue listing the items sorted by ascending order based on the total numbers in the right column. Like this:

Want Implementation Schedule (Sample Only)

Want	Required to Get	Ranking Total
Attend SEO free webinar	Do it myself	5
Listen to Napoleon Hill MP3	Do it myself	5
Remove phone from hook every Tuesday and Thursday from 7-9am to focus	Do it myself	5
Reduce alcohol to Friday only saving $200/mo	Do it myself	7
Upgrade website design	Contract Ned	11
Replace furnace	Pay ACME Co	12

Okay, you know the drill! It's your turn now. If you have put the thought and energy into the prior Lion Charges, completing this form should take you about five minutes.

Ready, GO!

My Official Want Implementation Schedule in Order from Lowest Total Rank to Highest

Want	Required to Get	Ranking Total

Good job again! You now have a road map of implementation steps to take to accomplish things in your business and life that you truly want. Now all we have to do is get your brain on board with really making it happen.

There is a big difference between people who know what they want (even if they know how to get there) and those that actually do GET what they want. There is one more Lion Charge for you to complete that will bring it all together. I'm going to give you the missing step for getting what you want.

LIONS ALWAYS WIN by Marty Dickinson

CHAPTER 5:
CONVERTING GETS INTO
HAVES

Knowing what you truly want and never receiving it can be even more painful than not discovering your wants to begin with. Maybe that is why so many of us never really take the time to figure out what we really want in our business and lives, because those wants, dreams and desires would seem so unattainable.

Do you know why a Lion nearly always achieves what they want (to catch their prey and enjoy a meal), but, in contrast, we do not get what we want? The answer is because we fail to make the decision that we simply WILL get what we want and not stop pursuing until we get it.

Earlier, I shared my love for Dr. Napoleon Hill, author of the 1937 published and best-selling book, *Think and Grow Rich*. Hopefully, I already made a strong enough case for you to get that book if you have never read it. Possibly, you are already into reading the first few chapters by now...for the first or the 20th time.

One of Dr. Hill's secrets is revealed early in his book (and also introduced earlier in this book), where he defines the importance of having what he calls *definiteness of purpose*. In modern-day language, that translates to being extremely specific about what you want and becoming obsessed to achieve it.

Quoting directly from the original version of *Think and Grow Rich:*

"Desiring riches with a state of mind that becomes an obsession, then planning definite ways and means to acquire riches, and backing those plans with persistence, which does not recognize failure, will bring riches."

If you have not yet read the book, don't get turned off by thinking Napoleon's book is only about money. The book title itself simply implies striving for richness in life. Money is one of many areas in our lives where richness is sought. The point is that definiteness of purpose, obsession with getting what you want, specific planning, and undying persistence will virtually assure your success in almost anything you strive to do or acquire.

My purpose for mentioning Dr. Hill's Definiteness of Purpose concept is an important one. After he describes the meaning of a Definiteness of Purpose, he suggests you write a Definiteness of Purpose statement on a piece of paper. He then challenges his readers to "recite it with *passion and conviction* when you wake up in the morning and when you go to bed each night" until your Want is realized.

However, I've always thought the word "purpose" is a bit misleading and limiting. Back in the 1930's and 40's when the book was getting its traction, a purpose was really any specific goal to achieve.

In present day 2020, a purpose has a much loftier and long-term meaning. Consider the "Want" of *closing a sale by the end of the day.* That's not a "purpose" by our standards today. It needs to happen today!

"I simply MUST *GET* a sale today!"

That's a "Get" statement.

I'm going to give you one final Lion Charge to help you get what you truly want by helping you to create a written Get Statement. You will read your Get Statement out loud with passion and conviction as soon as you get out of bed and before you crawl into bed to sleep—every day, every night—until your Get is realized.

Here is an example Get Statement that I helped one of my clients create just last month.

> *I am reading this statement out loud with complete passion and conviction as I am already reaching my objective to own an online business that is producing "inbox" money 24/7 at the rate of $25,000 per month between now and definitely no later than December 31, 2020.*
>
> *Yesterday's challenges, such as, lack of technical competency and funds with which to launch my businesses are already being overcome today by*

applying my highest skill power involving my business experiences and education, which is helping me be uniquely positioned to understand and recognize good opportunities when presented with them.

I feel self-pride and confidence and can actually see myself sitting on a beach of an Amazon River Basin island checking my account balance with a lightly tanned grin on my face as I realize my objective, to own an online business that is producing inbox money 24/7 and achieving the financial goal of $25,000 a month, has become a reality.

My plan to use my private placement that will capitalize my business is flawless and supported by my anxious desire to change occupations with the help of only myself and a virtual assistant. I am completely committed to give whatever it takes that I have available in trade for meeting my objective on-time without delay.

My brother, Joe, will monitor my progress and assure I take daily action toward my goal.

Still, I am leaving the opportunity open to change various parts of my plan that will allow me to own *an online business that is producing $25,000 a month mailbox money 24/7 more quickly and with even less effort than I imagined!*

My mind is completely closed to all negative and discouraging influences, including negative suggestions from relatives and friends.

Before you jump right into the Get Statement Lion Charge, I'd like to offer an experience I had personally with this process a few years ago to get something I wanted. Hopefully, this will inspire you to take your time and embrace the true power of these Lion Charges.

The True Power of Creating and Using a Get Statement

What you are about to go through as a process, probably for the first time, I have been using for several years now with most of my clients as well as for things I want myself and opportunities I wish to explore.

One day, I got together with one of my programmers and asked him to create an online tool for me that would automate some of the manual writing involved in creating a Get Statement. The Get Statement Generator is available to you in the bonus area described at the end of this book.

When he said it was ready for me to test, I went to the web-based location he provided. I clicked on drop-down buttons to choose selections for some answers to questions while other areas of the form allowed me to insert text of my own. The first question was, "What do you want?" My selection choices were mostly materialistic at that time. We were just testing after all.

So, I chose "Used Car" as my Want.

One of the questions asked for me to provide specific details to the Want. I entered the text "black SUV with tinted windows" and continued down the list.

Now, I was thinking at the time that I did need a new car. But, I figured the time when I really had to get a new car was a year away. I was wrong.

After finishing the questions, I clicked on the submit button and a beautiful Get Statement appeared on my screen in paragraph form. I read it

out loud (with passion and conviction) as my programmer buddy was on the phone with me.
I gave him a few tweaks to make and we hung up.

Less than five minutes later, the phone rang. Figuring it was my programmer saying he already had the changes in, I answered the phone by saying his name.

It wasn't my programmer on the phone at all! It was my wife. She was driving down a busy street where all the car dealerships are located and saw a BIG SALE sign out front with a bunch of girls in short shorts waving "for sale" signs. She asked if I would like to go look at cars.

Now, what are the chances of that? The fact that she called so soon after I read my Get Statement out loud is miraculous enough. But, even more amazing is that she would invite me to go anywhere close to a bunch of promotion models in short shorts jumping around!

When she got home, I jumped in her car and off we were to see the girls in short shorts…I mean, go car shopping.

When the salesman asked, "What are you looking

for in a car?" want to guess what my response was? "SUV, black, with tinted windows," of course.

Of all the used cars on that lot, only two were black SUVs with tinted windows. Only one of them happened to be within our price range.

We drove out of the parking lot that evening with my nice new "used" black Jeep with tinted windows. I still drive it today.

This Get Statement stuff is very powerful. Be careful with it! You have to take the time to consider what you really want and then put it into writing and start reciting it so that your brain understands you mean business!

If you are not willing to put in the time to craft Get Statements for what you want, then, you might want to ask yourself if you really have a strong enough desire to do whatever it takes to Get what you really Want.

If you know what you want and you are now driven more than ever to GET what you really WANT, then onward we go to the Lion Charge to create your Get Statement!

Lion Charge #12: Create Your Get Statement

Choose one specific "Want" from your Want list and answer the following 12 questions. Be as brief as you can, even to the point of using one-word answers. Be complete, however, in your responses incorporating required details.

Question #1: What Do You Want?

Question #2: By what realistic date will this Want be completed?

Question #3: Why is it so important to you that this Want is reached by this time limit?

Question #4: What ONE strength or skill will help you attain this Want?

Question #5: What limitations or challenges might stand in your way from achieving this Want?

Question #6: What is your current plan for attaining or acquiring the Want?

Question #7: Can you do this yourself or will you need volunteers, employees, or other helpers?

Question #8: What is your accountability partner's name who will help assure the Want is attained?

Question #9: What are you willing to give in exchange for getting the Want?

Question #10: What will you look like when you realize you have received the Want?

Question #11: Where will you be when you realize the Want is reached?

Question #12: How will you feel once you have achieved your goal?

Here is how my client completed these same questions, which supplied the answers used to create the Get Statement sample provided earlier.

Question #1: What do you want?
I want to own an online business that is producing inbox money 24/7! My specific goal is $25,000 per month.

Question #2: By what date do you realistically want this goal to be reached?
December 31, 2020.

Question #3: Why is it so important to get this Want by this time limit?
I am anxious to change occupations and cannot as things stand.

Question #4: What ONE strength will help you attain this Want?
I believe that with my store of business experiences and education, I am uniquely positioned to understand and recognize good opportunities when presented with them.

Question #5: What limitations or challenges might stand in your way from achieving this goal?
A lack of technical competency and funds with which to launch my businesses.

Question #6: Describe your current plan for attaining or acquiring the Want?
I am working on a private placement that will capitalize my ventures. I anticipate that I will get referrals from Marty Dickinson regarding the technical folks that I need.

Question #7: Can you do this yourself or will you need volunteers, employees, or other helpers?
I will need a virtual assistant to help with day-to-day management of subscribers.

Question #8: What is your accountability partner's name who will help assure the Want is attained?
My brother Joe.

Question #9: What are you willing to give in exchange for getting the Want?
Whatever it takes that I've got available.

Question #10: What will you look like when you realize you have received the Want?
I will have a lightly tanned grin on my face.

Question #11: Where will you be when you realize the Want is reached?
It has to be at the end of a month, as I have a monthly goal to reach. I will be sitting on the beach of an Amazon River Basin island checking my account balance.

Question #12: Describe how you will feel once you have achieved your goal.
Filled with self-pride and confidence knowing I would accomplish my goals all along.

Apply Your Answers to My "Get Statement" Formula

On a separate sheet of paper, I'm going to ask you to hand-write your Get Statement and fill-in the blanks as you go, with answers you provided in the Get Statement Questions above. Why write by hand? A proven connection exists between what you write with a pen-in-hand and your brain. Hand-writing your first Get Statement (then using the web-based tool) will introduce this message to your subconscious. Your subconscious will work with you to provide the right words to add so that the statement flows smoothly. Your subconscious wants you to Get what you Want!

I am reading this statement out loud with complete passion and conviction as I am already reaching my objective to **[Answer to Question #1]** *between now and definitely no later than* **[Answer to Question #2].**

Yesterday's challenges, such as **[Answer to Question #5]** *are already being overcome today by applying my highest skill or power being my* **[Answer to Question #4].**

I feel **[Answer to Question #12]** *and can actually*

see myself [Answer to Question #11] and [Answer to Question #10] as I realize my objective to [Answer to Question #1] has become a reality!

My plan to [Answer to Question #6] is flawless and supported by my [Answer to Question #3] with the help of only [Answer to Question #7]. I am completely committed to [Answer to Question #9] in trade for meeting my objective on-time without delay.

[Answer to Question #8] will monitor my progress and assure I take daily action toward my goal.

Still, I am leaving the opportunity open to change various parts of my plan that will allow me to [Answer to Question #1] more quickly and with even less effort than I imagined!

My mind is completely closed to all negative and discouraging influences, including negative suggestions from relatives and friends.

Once your Get Statement is complete, remember to read it out loud before you get into bed and right after you wake up in the morning. State each phrase with passion and conviction! Animate your voice with vocal variety like you really mean it! Convince your brain you really want to Get this Want! Continue with this reading process every day, every week, every month until the Want becomes a reality! Then, it's time to start on Getting your next Want!

 **Reminder: Use our web-based Get Statement Generator for free, found in the bonus area described at the end of this book.**

LIONS ALWAYS WIN by Marty Dickinson

CONCLUSION

How Exactly Does All This Help You Get What You Want?

Countless people go their whole adult lives being unhappy. They know they want something, but have no idea what that want is or how to discover it. Far more claw their way through life feeling like they have no options. Wants and Gets for those struggling through a daily existence seem about as far away as what an ant sees when it looks to the top of a mature redwood tree: Destination Impossible!

Lions are different. Lions know exactly what they want and wait patiently for the right opportunities to present themselves. When they do, there is no delay. Immediate action is taken and success is always achieved.

Lions Always Win

Whether you are already somewhat successful and searching for a balance between work and family or a chronic struggler trying to avoid bankruptcy, you have received a gift of process today. You have been introduced to a step-by-step sequence for evaluating where you are, discovering where you want to go, and a specific method to craft your plan to Get what you Want.

Your business and professional goals MUST be in line with your personal goals. If they are not, you could easily find that Chief Executive Bully (CEB) creeping into your business and life to create pain, doubt, and regret in your mind.

The result of no action can be lower than expected sales numbers, unpaid helpers and bills, and eventual layoffs and business closure.

You have likely heard the statistic that 95% of businesses will fail within three years. I suspect that more than half of those businesses will close their doors because the owner never took the time to figure out what he or she wanted and matched those wants with his or her skills or willingness to learn.

My bet is that 94% of that 95% of business owners who failed were never introduced to, or never took action with, writing a Get Statement and reciting it every day and night before going to bed and immediately after getting out of bed.

Employees in traditional jobs rarely make conscious plans for their upward mobility. They are happy with a positive review at the end of the year and a 2% raise, if they get an income increase at all.

Whether you work in corporate America or have chosen the path of entrepreneurism, YOU now have the opportunity to be one of the few to both succeed in your profession and get what you want. That level of fortune will require action and persistence, executed in a sequenced order.

Hire the right people to help you. Learn the tasks you have already determined you need to learn to help your business or career start or expand. Read your Get Statement aloud at least twice every day. In just a week or two (or even just a day or two possibly), ideas and opportunities will start placing themselves in front of you that will contribute toward getting what you want. All you have to do is recognize them and act on them!

Focus on one Get Statement at a time until you understand the true power of this process. Start with small Wants that can turn into Gets with few resources, little effort and fast results. Soon, you will be using the formula for every opportunity you wish to pursue.

Know too, that you can eventually use related Get Statements to acquire multiple categories of wants during the same time frame. For example, you might want to find a new girlfriend, lose 25 pounds, and repair a poor situation with a family member. These can all be combined into a single Get Statement.

Work the process, use the web-based Get Statement Generator frequently, and then let me know how your Wants and Gets have presented themselves to you. I truly want to know your results!

GAIN IMMEDIATE ACCESS TO THE BONUS AREA

- ✓ **Unlimited Use of the Get Statement Generator**
- ✓ **Pre-Configured Forms for All Lion Charges**
- ✓ **Supporting Videos**

ProduceMyBook.com/lionsbonusreg

[This offer is not publicly displayed on the ProduceMyBook.com website. It is only made available to those who have downloaded and/or purchased this book.]

ABOUT THE AUTHOR

Marty Dickinson hated his steady job selling accounting software. In 1996, he started a business called MusicMates.com to explore a different path. Six months later, he was offered a promotion at his job. In the same meeting, Marty resigned stating he was making too much money with the website that he could not afford to continue with the software company.

Participants in Music Mates began to ask Marty for help with their websites and internet strategy. One prospective client asked, "We'd like to hire you, but how do we know you'll be around in six months?" So, he started a web marketing agency called HereNextYear.com.

Nearly 25 years later, Marty and his team continue to work with U.S. entrepreneurs to help them *get what they want in business and life*. His 6-step A.C.T.I.O.N. system uses a blend of non-fiction book producing, speaker training, event facilitating, and internet marketing to achieve quantitative results.

Marty is a two-time co-author of *Web Marketing All-in-One for Dummies* (Wiley) and is the developer of the collaborative writing method course and services provided through ProduceMyBook.com.

.

If you enjoyed *Lions Always Win*, please take the time to tell others about your reading experience by providing an Amazon review. Very few people take the time to write reviews and they are so important to helping people make informed book buying decisions. Future readers, and this book's author, Marty Dickinson, would greatly appreciate it.

About Snowy Ridge Books

Being published and self-published book authors ourselves, we have experienced the same peaks and troughs of emotions and challenges as most authors.

We have developed a new way to develop non-fiction book content that completely removes the negative experiences associated with traditional writing.

Our secret sauce is what we call the D.O.N.E. Method, which enables authors to have books produced without ever actually writing or typing a single word of their initial manuscript.

While our books are published under the Snowy Ridge Books label, we provide training and support for our content development method through our sister website: ProduceMyBook.com

Produce My Book provides you with many benefits beyond traditional book publishing:

- Create your initial manuscript faster, usually within a week.

- Eliminate writer's block and enjoy producing content again!

- Reduce frustration by not having to type your manuscript.

- Save money by not having to hire a writing coach or ghost writer.

- Increase content quality by producing more complete content than you would generate on your own.

- Get e-book AND printed books without having to pay up-front printing costs.

- Enjoy the process because you are working closely, one-on-one, with our staff from beginning to launch.

Go to ProduceMyBook.com to watch our free signature talk describing our non-fiction book development process in detail.

If you would not normally take the time to write a book, or have tried to write a book for years, here is your chance to share your expert method with the world!

Snowy Ridge Books
PO Box 441024
Aurora, CO 80044-1024
https://SnowyRidgeBooks.com/
staff@SnowyRidgeBooks.com